AF489805

GEORGE WASHINGTON
THE FATHER OF HIS COUNTRY

History You Should Know
Children's History Books

Speedy Publishing LLC

40 E. Main St. #1156

Newark, DE 19711

www.speedypublishing.com

Copyright 2017

All Rights reserved. No part of this book may be reproduced or used in any way or form or by any means whether electronic or mechanical, this means that you cannot record or photocopy any material ideas or tips that are provided in this book

In this book, we're going to talk about the life of George Washington, the first President of the United States. So, let's get right to it!

GEORGE WASHINGTON

WHO WAS GEORGE WASHINGTON?

George Washington was the very first US President and he served two terms in office. As commander of the Continental Army, he led the colonists in a victorious battle against the British so that they could become an independent country, the United States of America. He helped to establish the role of the presidency for future presidents.

Washington was born in the colony of Virginia in 1732. His father passed away when he was only 11-years-old. He moved from household to household and stayed with his half brother, his mother, and other relatives at different times.

GEORGE WASHINGTON'S BIRTHPLACE

There's a legend about his coming-of-age years. As a youngster, Washington chopped down a cherry tree without permission. When he was questioned, he fessed up to his "crime" because he "couldn't tell a lie."

Certainly it was true that Washington grew up to be a leader and a man of solid character, but the story is most likely a fable written by the author who wrote his biography a year after Washington died.

GEROGE AND HIS MOTHER

By the time he was a teenager, Washington wanted to go out on his own. His plan was to join the British Royal Navy, but his mother pleaded with him not to go, so he stayed home instead. He was schooled in the usual reading, writing, and arithmetic and he also learned surveying, which is the process of land measurement.

Washington excelled at surveying and at the young age of 17 he was given the role as the surveyor for the county. His experience in the field led to his position as a major in the militia, a local military force in the colony of Virginia.

GEORGE WASHINGTON SURVEYING

FRENCH AND INDIAN WAR

THE FRENCH AND INDIAN WAR

The Seven Years' War was taking place in Europe during the years of 1754 through 1763. Great Britain and France were fighting over dominion of their colonies around the world. Land in North America was also up for grabs.

reat Britain, France, and Spain all had possession of different pieces of what is now the United States. A conflict began between France and Great Britain over the ownership of the Ohio River Valley. Robert Dinwiddie was the governor of the colony of Virginia at that time.

He sent Washington to warn the French not to overtake British holdings in the Ohio River Valley. He then promoted Washington to a lieutenant colonel. Along with his troops, Washington went forth to remove the French from Fort Duquesne.

ROBERT DINWIDDIE

The French fortified themselves and beat the Virginians in the ensuing battle. The French and Indian War was started over this event. The British sent troops to remove the French so they wouldn't expand into British-owned lands. Washington's leadership qualities were recognized and Dinwiddie promoted him to commander in chief of all the troops in the colony.

In 1758 he joined with British troops to successfully push the French out of Fort Duquesne. With that duty accomplished, Washington returned to his home at Mount Vernon and married the wealthy widow Martha Custis. He and his wife were both 27 years of age.

MARTHA CUSTIS

HOUSE OF BURGESSES IN THE CAPITOL
WILLIAMSBURG JAMES CITY COUNTY VIRGINIA

Washington's family and extended family were all influential in politics. In 1758, he was elected to the assembly in Virginia called the House of Burgesses. Two years later he began to serve as a judge in the county of Fairfax. He held that position for fourteen years and it shaped his views about the British.

The British were levying heavy taxes on the colonists. Although he had fought for the British, Washington opposed the unpopular Stamp Act, which was designed to tax almost all paper goods. One way that the colonists

tried to get Britain to change its taxation policies was to refuse to accept imported goods from Britain. Washington agreed with plans to prevent these imports in an effort to stop the heavy taxation.

CONTINENTAL CONGRESS

In 1774, the colonies sent representatives to an assembly, which they called the Continental Congress. Washington assisted in writing a resolution that would help to enforce a plan to prevent British imports. An additional proposal was that each county create a militia that was not under British control.

This means they would have some military power that was not controlled by the British. The colonies were beginning to get ready for what would become the Revolutionary War.

In 1775, Washington was the leader of the militia in Fairfax county. He was soon asked to command the militia of six other counties. By the time the Second Continental Congress met, Washington was elected to be commander in chief of all the armies of the colonies, now named the Continental Army. The French supplied troops in 1788 and Washington was now leading the forces of the colonies and the French troops in the Revolutionary War.

CONTINENTAL CONGRESS COMMITTEE OF FIVE

GEORGE DURING AMERICAN REVOLUTION

At that time, Britain was a major military power. Washington had a difficult task ahead. At the beginning, his army was an unorganized group of farmers who had few skills as soldiers. It's a testament to Washington's commanding leadership that he was able to keep them motivated to continue to fight.

The Revolutionary War was fought over six years. Washington led the troops to many victories including the famous Delaware River crossing on Christmas Day. Ultimately, the Revolutionary War was won by the colonists and the British were defeated in Virginia at the city of Yorktown in October of 1781. The new country called the United States of America was born.

BATTLE OF TRENTON

GENERAL GEORGE WASHINGTON

During the Revolution, Washington continued to grow as a leader, administrator, and politician. Even though the United States did not yet have a formal government in position, he took on the role of "chief executive" of the newly forming country very early on.

When the war was over, Washington went back to his lands at Mount Vernon. He and his wife had a huge estate with many slaves because at that time it

wasn't illegal to have slaves. Washington would eventually free his slaves in his final will and testament.

In 1787, a Federal Convention was held. The goal of the Convention was to agree upon the basic legislation of the new government, namely the Constitution.

PHILADELPHIA CONVENTION IN 1787

GEORGE WASHINGTON

FIRST AMERICAN PRESIDENT

The final battle of the American Revolutionary War was in Yorktown but the war didn't officially come to a close until 1783 when the Treaty of Paris was agreed upon. It was six years later when Washington was chosen by the representatives of the former colonies to be the first President of the United States.

The colonies had just gained their independence from the British king, but despite this, they decided that the new President should have a lot of power. Washington was the only president in America's history who was elected unanimously, which essentially means that every single representative voted for him.

INDEPENDENCE DAY

GEORGE WASHINGTON AT PHILADELPHIA CONVENTION

Once Washington was in office he helped to mold the Constitution into a living document that was useful for governing a new nation. A Bill of Rights, which listed the rights that every citizen would have, was created and added to that living document. The three branches of government and the cabinet were formed.

During this time, there was an ongoing debate about how strong the federal government should be. Thomas Jefferson, who was secretary of state, and Alexander Hamilton, who was secretary of the Treasury, were part of Washington's cabinet and they were on opposite sides of this debate.

THOMAS JEFFERSON

THE JEFFERSONIAN DEMOCRACY

Jefferson wanted the states to hold most of the power while Hamilton favored a strong central government. Those who favored a strong central government were called Federalists. Those who opposed were called anti-Federalists or Republicans, although they were not the same as the Republican political party today.

Washington thought of retiring at the end of his first term but both Hamilton as well as Jefferson convinced him to stay in office for a second term. In 1793, the unrest in Europe became a pressing issue for the new nation. The French were fighting with Great Britain and they sent Edmond Genet to the US.

EDMOND GENET

GEORGE WASHINGTON

Clearly, the French were hoping to get the aide of the new country in their fight against the British. However, Washington was hoping that the United States would have a peaceful beginning and not become entangled in Europe's squabbles.

Washington issued a statement that the United States would remain neutral. It was discovered that Genet had allowed French pirates access to ports in America. He had also coordinated expeditions into both Louisiana and Florida. These states were not yet part of the United States, but Genet had caused a huge problem.

WEST INDIES FRENCH RULE

Britain retaliated by taking control over neutral ships that were doing commerce with the islands of the West Indies under French rule. Washington dispatched John Jay to settle these lingering problems between the British and the US government. Though the treaty was not popular it kept the new country out of war.

WASHINGTON MONUMENT

At the time of his death in 1799, the US Congress acted to create a monument to him in what was now the nation's capital. The Washington Monument is a towering tribute to this great leader who is known as the father of the United States.

WASHINGTON MONUMENT

Awesome! Now you know more about the life and achievements of the first US president, George Washington. You can find more History books from Baby Professor by searching the website of your favorite book retailer.

Visit

BABY PROFESSOR
EDUCATION KIDS

www.BabyProfessorBooks.com

to download Free Baby Professor eBooks and view
our catalog of new and exciting Children's Books

www.ingramcontent.com/pod-product-compliance
Lightning Source LLC
Chambersburg PA
CBHW080513180726
48000CB00029BA/3038